SUN 'N FUN

SUN 'N FUN

FLORIDA'S AVIATION EXTRAVAGANZA

Geoff Jones

Front cover Declared best fighter at Sun 'n Fun in 1989 was Jim Priebe's P-51D Mustang *Glamorous Jen*, which is based at Findlay, Ohio

Back cover Cessna's big bird, the 195: Tom Hulls' immaculate Grand Champion classic, N1504D reposes at Lakeland in 1989. The 300 hp Jacobs performed perfectly during the flight from Hollywood, Maryland

Title Page For many of the 250,000 visitors to Sun 'n Fun this palm tree shaded sign heralded the end of the road and the start of the fun. Sub-tropical Florida is at its best in the spring, when the state enjoys reasonable temperatures and almost guaranteed sunshine. Throw in thousands of sport planes and it's no wonder that this EAA fly-in has become so popular

Contents page The futuristic Cirrus VK-30 made its airshow debut in 1988 after a six-hour flight from Baraboo, Wisconsin. One year later, thousands of hours of development work completed, the Cirrus' design team (the average age of which is a youthful 27), started to take orders for kits. A deposit of $500 secures a delivery position, but a complete VK-30 costs up to $100,000

Right An Avid Flyer mounted on a trailer in the parking lot of a Lakeland motel—have airplane, will travel!

Published in 1990 by Osprey
Publishing Limited
59 Grosvenor Street,
London W1X 9DA
© Geoff Jones

British Library Cataloguing in Publication Data

    Jones, Geoffrey P. (Geoffrey Peter), 1928–
    Sun 'n Fun.
    1. Sport flying
    I. Title
    629.133'347

ISBN 0–85045–968–0

Editor Dennis Baldry
Page design Simon Ray-Hills
Printed in Hong Kong

Introduction

First held in 1974 as a regional fly-in by the Lakeland, Florida Chapter of the Experimental Aircraft Association (EAA) for sport aviation enthusiasts, it was named the Mid-Winter Sun 'n Fun the following year and by 1978 the event had become the second largest fly-in in the USA.

In 1980 the event was held in March instead of January and the growth of the week-long fly-in began to escalate to the proportions which are described and illustrated in this book. The 10th anniversary Sun 'n Fun in 1984 saw 480 show aircraft register and a general attendance of over 100,000 people for the first time. Permanent facilities for the fly-in at Lakeland airport were then starting to appear or enter the planning stage.

The year 1988 saw yet another date change, this time to mid-April to take advantage of slightly better weather and improved accommodation for the many thousands of visitors who were now converging on Lakeland each year from every US State and 37 other countries world-wide.

Sun 'n Fun is big, but not too big. It's still fun and, blended with traditional Southern hospitality, the event has rapidly established itself as one of the world's premier aviation 'happenings'.

The photographs in this book were taken between 1986–89 using Pentax equipment and Kodachrome 64 film.

Geoff Jones, Guernsey, Channel Islands, January 1990

The words Sun 'n Fun are copyright and are used in this book with the kind permission of Sun 'n Fun EAA Fly-In, Inc.

Contents

Homebuilts & Kitplanes

April, season of mists and mellow fruitfullness? A sunrise study of Mark Brown's two-seat Pulsar composite kitplane, a development of his successful single-seat Starlite design. By 1989's Sun 'n Fun Brown had taken orders for 45 Pulsar kits and had delivered 18—The Pulsar's 125 mph cruise at 3.8 gph from a 65 hp Rotax 532 puts the performance of a Cessna 150 completely in the shade

Above Flown on the long flight from Ontario, Canada by its designer, Peter Cowan, the Cekady—a hybrid homebuilt featuring Cessna 170/172 parts matched to a homebuilt steel-tube fuselage—has flown equipped with floats, skis as well as wheels since it made its maiden flight in 1982. The plentiful supply of used Cessna parts should allow a builder to complete his Cekady quickly and cheaply

Right At 2500 ft over Florida with the morning cloud layer burning off, the perfect backdrop for our Pulsar camera ship to formate on Peter Cowan flying his Cekady. Half an hour later re-joining the Lakeland airport pattern to land at Sun 'n Fun the tranquility was shattered as we became No 42—or was it No 52?—to land on one of the three parallel strips in use to get the busy opening day flood of aircraft on the ground before the airport closed for the afternoon airshow

Left Observant onlookers will see the initials of the builder of this Smyth Sidewinder incorporated in the aircraft's colour scheme. 'HF' is Harry Flood, who flew this racy homebuilt from Wisconsin to attend the 1986 Sun 'n Fun

Above Basic but neat cockpit detail of Harry Flood's Smyth Sidewinder—looks like the lounge armchairs may have been used to provide the upholstery!

Left 'I'm a book-keeper not a qualified aeroplane builder', declared Warren Jolly, from Mount Vernon, Illinois when he made only his second flight away from his home base to attend the 1989 Sun 'n Fun. His modesty did not influence the EAA judges who declared his Bakeng Duce the 'Best High Wing Experimental' at the fly-in

Above Superb workmanship is evident everywhere in Warren Jolly's tandem-seat Bakeng Duce homebuilt. His 'Rules To Remember' placard on the cockpit wall is a sobering reminder to many a bold pilot, *'Number of Landings Must Always Equal Number of Take Offs—DON'T DO NOTHIN DUMB'*

In 1986 the Prescott Pusher was heralded as the quintessential homebuilt design—by 1988 and millions of dollars of development money later, the dream had foundered and kits were no longer available

Morrey Hummel's diminutive Hummel Bird single-seater is built from pop-rivetted alloy, has an 18-ft wing span and is powered by 'half a Volkswagen engine'—despite this half-measure just 28 hp gives the Bird a creditable 105 mph cruise

Since the advent of composite aircraft construction there have been many pretenders to the kitplane 'throne'. One of the original companies to have stood the test of time is Stoddard-Hamilton with their Glasair range of kitplanes—Sun 'n Fun's line-up of Glasairs grows every year

Left Stoddard-Hamilton's Glasair III prototype made its Sun 'n Fun debut in 1987 setting new standards for kitplanes with its 282 mph cruise on 75% power. A regular at Sun 'n Fun ever since, it is aerobated by Bob Herendeen and has accumulated over 1000 hours since its first flight in July 1986

Above The ultimate Glasair, this turbo-powered Glasair III flown at Sun 'n Fun '89 is marketed as the Arocet AT-9 Stalker. Not intended for the one-off homebuilt/kitplane market, its 420 shp Allison and 366 mph cruise cut an immediate niche for the AT-9 as a military trainer

Left Glaisair TD—'tail dragger', one of the earlier and still highly popular Glasair designs, moves off Lakeland's runway past Roger Holler's beautifully restored, 1943 vintage DC-3, just in after the short hop from its base at Orlando Executive airport

Above 1989's Sun 'n Fun was to have been the venue where Dave Riley put himself and the Raiderhawk I into the speed record books—an engine failure on take-off put paid to that dream. With a 417 hp Lycoming from a Piper Navajo and a VP prop 'blended' to the fuselage of a Midget Mustang, the aircraft, built by Jim Thompson, was perhaps a tad over-ambitious

Left Sun 'n Fun is invaded each year by the epitome of the modern homebuilt, the Vari and LongEzes, designed by the legendary Burt Rutan. This is part of 'Eze-Street '89' Florida style

Above Up, up and away—as dawn brightens into morning a massed hot air balloon ascent heralds the opening day of Sun 'n Fun in 1989

25

Nearly there with only a few feet to touchdown on Lakeland's 09 runway for this composite homebuilt, the Viking Dragonfly. Looking very much like a QAC Quickie, the Dragonfly differs in that it's a plans-built design

One of Sun 'n Fun's vast army of voluntary helpers, this biker guides a pair of Rutan Defiants to their tie-down position under threatening skies

Dan Maher's Velocity made its debut at Sun 'n Fun in 1985. A composite
kitplane, it takes the Rutan VariEze concept to the realms of a four-seat, single-
engined canard. Maher started working with composites by building fibreglass
off-shore racing boats in Florida. 'How is a boat guy able to come up with an
airplane like this in such a short time?' asked one learned aviation journalist. 'He
doesn't know any better', was the terse reply

Above A tandem, two-seat homebuilt design of metal construction, the Vans RV-4 is an extremely popular homebuilt aircraft with over 2000 sets of plans sold; 150 RV-4s are now flying with a further 900 under construction. Designer Richard Van Grunsven got something right!

Right After the success of the Vans RV-4, Van Grunsven turned his attention to a more sociable version, the RV-6, a side-by-side two-seater. Each year since this RV-6 prototype first flew in June 1986 he has made the 3000 mile trans-Continental flight from his home in Oregon for Sun 'n Fun

Left Homebuilts in the foreground—
antiques and classics beyond at
1988's fly-in, part of the 902
'showplane' attendance that year and
helping towards the staggering total
of 20,830 aircraft movements during
the week-long event

Above A Hatz Biplane makes the
long taxi to its parking spot amongst
the other homebuilts at 1987's Sun 'n
Fun—the Hatz design dates back to
1959 when John D Hatz started
construction of this basic, tandem-
seat, steel tube fuselage/wooden
wing design with an 85 hp
Continental engine

George Ola from Arcadia in Florida designed and built this one-off wood and fabric homebuilt based on the 1920's Travelair biplane designs. Much smaller of course, what else could it be but a Tiny Travelair?

European homebuilt designs at US fly-ins are rare. An exception is Marcel Jurca's tandem-seat design, the MJ-5 Sirocco. Two examples of this attractive French design attended Sun 'n Fun in 1988

The sleek lines of the reverse stagger wing and aerofoil-shaped fuselage distinguish the Sorrell SNS-7 Hiperbipe—a design which has turned heads at EAA fly-ins ever since the prototype was awarded the 'Outstanding New Design' award at Oshkosh in 1973

Forrest Molberg flew this Swearingen SX-300 to Sun 'n Fun in 1988 on behalf of Jaffe Aircraft Corporation, who were negotiating sales of the type in its turboprop-powered development form as the SA-32T military trainer. Demonstrations to the USAF were also reported but not confirmed until the tragic news broke that Molberg had been killed on 9 January 1989 flying this SX-300 near Wright-Patterson AFB, Ohio when the starboard wing detached

One of the long-time classics from the US homebuilt scene is the Thorpe T-18, John Thorpe's side-by-side, metal design, the first example of which flew in May 1964. Normally a fixed gear design, this unusual retractable gear version appeared at the 1988 fly-in

This aircraft looks as if it means business—Freedom Master's FM-2 Air Shark amphibian with its pylon mounted 200 hp Lycoming approaches the camera. A four-seat kitplane, assembled from pre-moulded composite parts, several Air Sharks have now been completed

Left Dick Moore from Florida completed the first 'production' version of this futuristic looking Canadian amphibian design, the Seawind 2000. Another four-seat, composite kitplane, 90 kits of which had been sold prior to Sun 'n Fun in 1989, 'without any advertising at all', claimed the ebullient Seawind salesmen

Above Almost like a glider in construction and looks, the Seawind 2000 has a 200 horse Lycoming mounted above and behind the cockpit *a la* Trislander. The spacious four-seat cockpit has dual controls and exudes an air of refinement

Left Dan Denney has survived! One of the many upstart designer/builders of Cub-a-like ultralights during the 1980's, his Kitfox, two-seat, Rotax-powered kitplane continues to sell well throughout the world. The wry smile of success comes from many years of hard work

Above Those big tundra tyres and high lift wings make the Denney Kitfox a great go-anywhere performer be it fitted with tyres, floats or skis. Kitfoxes have been sold in their hundreds to civilian builders, but the design is also finding a ready market with some third-world air forces and government agencies from Mexico to the Philippines

At Sun 'n Fun's regular 'hands on' workshop training sessions you too can learn to make parts for the Zenair CH-701. Out on the airfield this STOL two-seater made demo flights from Sun 'n Fun's special grass strip with designer Chris Heintz at the controls

Ultralights

Left A 1989 Sun 'n Fun debutant was Randy Schlitter's new aspirant in the two-seat trainer market, the Rans S-6 Cyote II. Schlitter quotes a price of $12,500 for a basic Cyote II kit which includes the Rotax 503 engine

Below Cavorting Cub-a-likes keep the crowds lining the grass ultralight strip entertained. The yellow aircraft is the Mosler Super Pup, a clip-wing single-seater, and beyond is the new tandem two-seat Mosler N-3-2 Pup, both powered by the lightweight Mosler 4-stroke engine operating at an affordable $2 per hour

Left End of the trail from Tennessee to Florida as the Loehle Enterprises 5151
Mustang arrives. This wood/fabric kitplane, resembling a P-51 Mustang, first
sold for $5151. The price has increased but the designation's stuck

Above Part of the light plane revolution that started with powered hang-
gliders and helped by the availability of new high power-to-weight ratio
engines such as the Rotax and KFM, ultralights have come a long way in the
last ten years. A sophisticated 1989 newcomer in this category is the Rans S-10
Sakota, a side-by-side two-seat variant of the earlier single seat S-9. These form
part of a whole range of kitplanes designed and developed by Randy Schlitter
at Hayes in Kansas

Above The flag on the tail gives away the nationality of this Spirit biplane. Yet another Rotax-powered ultralight despite designer Darryl Murphy's cunningly designed cowling. A tandem, two-seat, all-metal constructed kitplane that weighs less than 400 lbs empty, it provides modest fun flying performance for those pilots whose pocket won't stretch to a Pitts or Christen Eagle

Right In the late 1980's most of the action in new designs moved from Sun 'n Fun's homebuilt area to the ultralight area. Carlson Aircraft's Sparrow II was unveiled at Sun 'n Fun in 1989, yet another two-seat, Rotax-powered kitplane. Here the Sparrow II sneaks past the trees to land on Sun 'n Fun's special ultralight grass strip on the southern perimeter of Lakeland airport

EXPERIMENTAL

March 1987 at Sun 'n Fun saw the debut of this somewhat ungainly looking two-seat ultralight biplane, the Kelly D-11. A natural development of the earlier single-seat Kelly D that first flew in 1981, the D-11 is powered by the almost obligatory Rotax engine fitted to this class of aircraft

From 500 ft the Sun 'n Fun ultralight strip and tented village to the left looks quite small. Next to this is the aircraft camping area accommodating over 600 units in 1989 and, spilling out of the trees beyond, the RV's and tents of the main camp site where 4000 visitors lived throughout the week of the fly-in

Above There's colourful conviviality and plenty of activity from dawn till dusk in Sun 'n Fun's ultralight area. Flying demonstrations to potential customers are frequent. Each day around lunch time and before the main airshow gets under way, the various ultralight manufacturers put their products through their paces

Right Looking down on a Sparrow. Some of the ultralight exhibitors chalets with Carlson Aircraft's single-seat Sparrow (left) and the Kolb Twin Star (right), and beyond row upon row of visiting aircraft of all shapes and sizes. The hangars of Lakeland Municipal Airport's resident FBO's on the north side of the airfield are visible in the distance

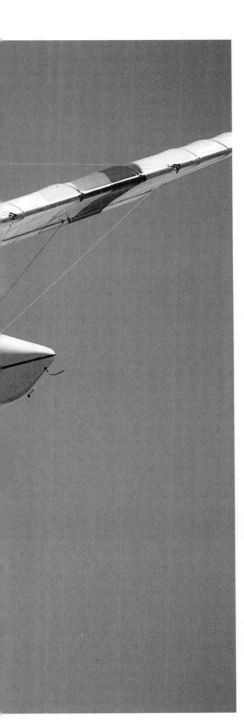

Left In the warm Florida sun in tee-shirts and crash helmets what better way to fly than in the open cockpit of a Maxair Drifter. There are now five versions of the Drifter kit available from Maxair at their Lake Wales headquarters close to Lakeland with 1562 delivered to customers by the time of 1989's Sun 'n Fun

Below Sun and not so much fun! What started as an enjoyable flying demonstration could have ended in disaster when this Maxair Drifter landed long on the ultralight strip. The unwelcome and muddy ditch and the end of the strip was waiting to gobble him up but fortunately the occupants walked away with only damaged pride, a bent aircraft and laundry bills for their muddy Levi's

The most recent addition to Homer Kolb's range of homebuilt ultralight kits is the single-seat Kolb Firestar. The kit comes with a completely pre-welded chrome-molybdenum steel tube fuselage and differs from other Kolb designs in having a central joystick instead of a sidestick. The Rotax 377 engine will push the Firestar along at 50 mph; it can take off from a 100 ft strip and stalls at 25 mph

Canadian participation at Sun 'n Fun is growing. Amongst the new types exhibited in 1989 was the Kestrel Hawk designed by David Saunders. In Canada it comes within their ultralight criteria but in the USA it's an Experimental or homebuilt. The prototype of this unusual two-place, metal, biplane first flew in California in 1986 and by 1989 ten factory completed aircraft had been delivered to customers. Kit Hawks will soon be available and the aircraft has since been flown on both floats and skis

Above Glossy paintwork and fancy instrument panels are fine but it's always useful to know what makes up the bones of a homebuilt. First Strike Aviation weren't afraid to reveal all in demonstrating this part-completed example of their Supercat at Sun 'n Fun in 1988

Right Before and after. A simple welded steel-tube fuselage frame, the upper part of which is covered in light alloy and the remainder Dacron fabric. If it all looks fairly straightforward that's what Flightworks Corporation expect. The Capella's a neat single-seat design, the completed example here having received an 'Honorable Mention' for builder J Reid-Howell at Oshkosh in 1988

Warbirds

One of the largest aircraft on 1989 Sun 'n Fun's warbird row appears through the ethereal light in much the same way as it must have done during its service career with the Royal Canadian Air Force's No 161 Sqn when flying during 1944–45 from Yarmouth, Nova Scotia and Torbay, Newfoundland. The PBY-5A Catalina is now based at Hobby airport, Houston, Texas with Tailwind Aviation and was flown to Sun 'n Fun by Don Wells and Ernesto Morales. Now N5404J, it was purchased from Meldy Fernandez in Guatemala City as TG-BIV in 1988

Above Catalina pilot's eye view of warbird row. The port Pratt & Whitney R-1830 Twin Wasp radial was spewing oil after the flight from Texas, a minor irritation compared to the blown starboard engine which the crew had to deal with during a flight from Guatemala City in November 1986. The pilot had failed to drain the water from the fuel tanks before the flight

Left Catalina cockpit—basic is not the word. Stripped of most equipment the flight from Houston to Florida was flown VFR following the Gulf coast, a long flight cruising at only 130 mph, compounded by a headwind most of the way

Sweet Charlotte from Tulsa, Oklahoma, is a Lockheed Lodestar, the civil development of the Hudson, with modified nose, Wright Cyclones and Hamilton Standard props

Military mix at Sun 'n Fun '87 with John Silberman's characteristic cat motif on the nose of his P-38 Lightning. A T-6 Texan taxies in behind and to the right is the Boeing B-17G N93102, *Nine 'o Nine* owned by the Collings Foundation from Stow, Massachusetts but based at Tom Reilly's Kissimmee, Florida Flying Tigers Warbird Air Museum, until its crash later in 1987

Warbirds come in all shapes and sizes and at 1989's Sun 'n Fun 132 registered. Reserve Grand Champion was this Fairchild PT-23A flown by Harland Avezzie from Westfield, Massachusetts. The PT-23 was one of the US Army's standard basic trainers based on the PT-19 but fitted with a 220 hp Continental radial engine in place of the original in-line Ranger for improved performance. By the time production of the PT-23 began the blue and yellow colours of PT-19's had been replaced by silver overall

Above One of the commonest aircraft types on warbird row is the North American T-6 Texan. Over 20,000 were built, including Canadian and Australian licence-built derivatives . A good T-6 can be picked up through the columns of *Trade-A-Plane* for around $90,000—but the fuel bill's likely to be a bit heavier than your average Piper or Cessna

Right For any warbird enthusiast with a camera, an early morning call and a quiet uninterrupted stroll down warbird row will soon banish any lingering sleepiness. Caught with the remnants of a heavy overnight dew, this T-6, NX1467 awaits the crowds

Left This DHC-1 Chipmunk 2 visited Sun 'n Fun in 1988 and '89 flown by Mike Lyon. Immediately distinguished from its British-built namesake by the clear blown canopy, the Chipmunk was the first aircraft designed and built by de Havilland Canada and replaced the legendary Tiger Moth in RCAF service. The prototype first flew in May 1946

Above Mike Lyon fuels up Bill Rose's DHC-1 Chipmunk, a Canadian variant with the blown bubble canopy. Lyon has retired from full time commercial flying with his log book bulging with thousands of commercial hours flying for PanAm, Air Congo and most recently the DC-8 operated by Orbis as a flying optical surgery

Left After the T-6 the most common type on warbird row in the North American T-28, appropriately a type that was designed to replace it. As the Trojan it was used extensively by the USAF as a trainer and also saw active service as a close-support aircraft with the French in Indochina and Algeria and the South Vietnamese Air Force.

Inset Every year at Sun 'n Fun members of the Canadian Warplane Heritage museum from Hamilton, Ontario fly some of their aircraft south to the spring-time Florida sun. In 1989 it was the turn of their T-28C *Old Ugly* to make the trip, now smartly finished in US Navy colours and part of the final batch of T-28's built with a more powerful engine and capable of carrier operations. CWH's aircraft, s/n 146255 was built in 1956 and saw service in Zaire and Vietnam before joining the collection in 1987

Above Trojan horses: an immaculate T-28B in authentic USAF markings on long finals, flaps extended

In the colours of a US Navy Douglas A-1E Skyraider from the Naval Air Station Pensacola, Florida, this Sun 'n Fun warbird N62466 flown by Peter Thelen from Ft Lauderdale, Florida exhibits its folded wings, saving space on the flight-line and shading the cockpit. The A-1E was dubbed a 'multiplex' version in production, Douglas starting with a basic 'chassis' with different variants emerging at the end of the line,—this version was a three-seat shipboard early warning aircraft and part of a total production run of 3180 aircraft

Above Contrasting with the heavier metal, this replica First World War Fokker D.VII is the work of Bob Iseman from Clearwater in Florida. Powered by a cleverly concealed 175 hp Ranger engine the aircraft first flew in April 1985 and has been a Sun 'n Fun regular since

Right When the starter of this P-51 Mustang wouldn't engage a squirt of WD-40 did the trick. *Glamorous Glen III* may be the name of this P-51D but the glamour fades for owners Ed and Connie Bowlin when flight-line maintenance is required. The markings of this Mustang N551CB are those of the aircraft flown in World War 2 by Brigadier General Chuck Yeager

Taxying in at Sun 'n Fun '89 after the flight from Fayetville, Georgia, this P-51D NL6320T/44-74497 is an ex-RCAF aircraft now preserved and flown by Heritage Aircraft Inc

Each year at Sun 'n Fun many of the warbird pilots take a mid-week break and fly north at the invitation of Jimmy and Dick Leeward to their Leeward Air Ranch near Ocala, Florida. In the informal almost garden party atmosphere of the Ranch the pilots of these three P-51 Mustangs found that compared to Sun 'n Fun, anything goes

Inset Four Mustangs in a 'tête à tête' on the front lawn of some up-market real estate at the Leeward Air Ranch. In 1982 the first of these plots were sold off for $20-30,000 as the finishing touches were put to the Ranch's 5000 ft reinforced grass runway. The Leeward's stress to any potential occupant of a property or plot on the Ranch that it's a Sport Aviation Community—aircraft ownership in itself won't get you in, it has to be a sport aircraft. Looking out on this feast of Mustangs is the occupant of the white building, none other than the legendary Steve Wittman who despite his 85 years can still be regularly seen at the Ranch putting air beneath his tyres

Right Main Street Leeward and what's that damn machine just flashed past the window? Such might be the reaction of the occupant of the large cream coloured mansion as Jim Priebe zooms low along the runway in his P-51D *Glamorous Jen*. This reaction is unlikely though, the occupant in question being J Dawson Ransom, son of East Anglian agricultural machinery manufacturer, founder of Philadelphia based commuter airline Ransome Airlines and former PanAm executive. He's retired to Leeward to lavish care and attention on his orange and white CASA 1-131 just visible in his 'garage'

Above Cameras click as Jim Priebe does a low level fly-past at Leeward Air Ranch in his P-51 *Glamorous Jen*, other assorted warbird visitors up for the day and the open air barbecque forming an appropriate back-drop

A Sun 'n Fun prizewinner in 1987, Dan McCue slows to taxi speed after landing at Leeward Air Ranch in his unique NA-50 replica. Only seven NA-50's were originally built, the North American Company coming up with the design by modifying their successful AT-6 Texan through the addition of a Wright Cyclone 1820–77 engine—the shape of the airframe was also altered slightly. McCue had his NA-50 conversion done to his specifications, completed in 1986 and fitted with the larger Pratt & Whitney R1340-61 together with a full oxygen system

Left Leeward Air Ranch is located in undulating ranching country, a pleasant change from the almost dead flat Florida countryside around Lakeland. During 1989's warbird fly-in to the Ranch a newcomer had just arrived, N99426, an On Mark Marksman conversion of the Douglas A-26C Invader owned by Buddy Head and Vern Thorpe, dwarfing more modest visitors

Above Small and unassuming yet still true warbirds, the military liaison aircraft are lined up at Leeward Air Ranch whilst their pilots gorge steaks, chicken breasts, corn on the cob and lavish helpings of beans at the barbecque organized by the Leewards each year during Sun 'n Fun. An Aeronca L-16 in front with other Aeronca models behind, the row completed by an ex-Israeli AF Dornier Do 27 N77AX.

Jet warbirds are becoming more prevalent at Sun 'n Fun. With the import of several ex-Finnish AF Fouga Magisters to the USA a line up of three could be seen. One was the all black 'Dog Whistle' N204DM owned by Rick Korff from Niagara Falls seen here about to touch down on Lakelands 09 runway. Korff also regularly flies a Mustang, *Six Shooter*, to Sun 'n Fun

Antiques & Classics

Right Like the de Havillands were to private flying between the wars in Britain and the Commonwealth, in the USA there were the wonderful Waco's. Seen arriving in 1988 is N1125, a 1930 Waco RNF, a three-place with a 50% stagger between the wings. The 125 hp Warner engine is shrouded with the optional speed ring

Below It's difficult to see where you're going when taxying tail-draggers like the Waco RNF. The front cockpit passenger stretches up to look over the cowling and shout directions to the pilot who is weaving the aircraft down the taxi-way. This Model 'F' sold for $4250 when new and the Weaver Aircraft Company built 250, selling them through a chain of 35 distributors and 300 dealers. It was Sam Junkin and Clayton Brukner who first formed the company in the winter of 1920, but 'Buck' Weaver negotiated the financing and it was agreed to call it the Weaver Aircraft Company—shortened to Waco—by mutual consent

Top left Parked by the trees at the west end of Lakeland airport during 1986's Sun 'n Fun was this Waco DSO NC8558, maintained at the time by the Lakeland Aviation Corporation. This model dates from 1928, the DSO being characterized by its straight wing and 150 hp Hisso, although this one has been converted to Waco ASO standard with a 220 hp Wright

Bottom left All shined up and ready to go. To the north of Orlando, not far from Lakeland, Bob White runs a small aircraft restoration facility which specializes in refurbishing Waco's. At his small grass airfield, called what else but Bob White Field, his Waco CTO NC7446 is ready for its Sun 'n Fun debut in 1989 when White was awarded prizes for the 'Best Silver Age 1928–32 Antique' and for the 'Best Open Cockpit Antique' with this aircraft. It's finished in the colours of a Northwest Airways Waco—Northwest bought nine in 1929 to inaugurate night mail services between Minneapolis/St Paul and Chicago

Right A pleasant and rare sight at 1986's Sun 'n Fun, this Naval Aircraft Factory N3N-3 primary trainer N45192, had by 1989 forsaken the USA and had been exported to Great Britain. It is now owned by Pete Treadaway who bases the aircraft, now G-ONAF, at North Weald

One of Sun 'n Fun's regulars is this immaculate Travel Air 2000 owned by Rod Spanier. Only a handful still exist out of around 600 built. It was the Travel Air Manufacturing Co's first production aeroplane, the company having been founded by Walter Beech and Clyde Cessna, an enviable parentage

No 27 on the pre-flight checks is 'Ensure the anchor is stowed and secure'. A remarkable stainless steel aerial yacht, the Fleetwing Seabird dates from 1936, when they sold for an expensive $20,000—only six were built. Only two survive and this one, NC19191, graced Sun 'n Fun in 1989. The clinical starkness of the Seabird's fuselage beckons the onset of some sun and warmth

Blake Oliver gets the camera's clicking as he taxies his rare Fleetwing F.5 Seabird in at 1989's Sun 'n Fun. The aircraft is based at Daytona Beach in north Florida. To complement the gleaming spot-welded stainless steel airframe, Oliver had additional metal to carry back home in the shape of his award for 'Reserve Grand Champion'. That big pylon-mounted engine above the fuselage is a 330 hp Jacobs L-6 radial

Out for an airing is one of the exhibits from the Sun 'n Fun Air Museum, Ryan ST3KR Recruit N53189—a customized PT-22—with palm trees providing a rare spot of shade as the crowd thrills to the sight of Bob Herendeen hurling the Glasair III through the Lakeland skies

Top right Ron Tesierman's
Monocoupe 90 sparkles in the
sunlight amongst the other antiques
and classics at 1988's Sun 'n Fun. The
aircraft, built in 1948, is a hybrid,
being one of only eleven Monocoupe
90AL's built post-war—they were
fitted with 115 hp Lycomings as
standard but Tesierman, from
Roanoake, Virginia, has rebuilt and
reworked this one, preferring a larger
150 hp Lycoming instead

Left NC34825 arrives at Sun 'n Fun
1989 from Naples, Florida, on short
finals for the grass strip 09 that
complements the main runway 09
and the parallel taxiway 09—all of
which are used simultaneously for
landing aircraft during busy spells. A
Rearwin 8135 Cloudster, one of only
eight survivors from the 125 built in
1939/40, is flown by Joseph and
Alex Garland and rewarded them
with the 'Best Monoplane' award

In the evening sun during 1987's fly-
in, this Ranger-engined Fairchild 24R
provides a pleasing sight with the
rows of homebuilts already bedded
down for the night beyond

Far from the madding crowd at the Leeward Air Ranch, one of its many rare and beautiful residents is this Aeronca C-3 Collegian, NC12496, dating from 1932. In the Sun 'n Fun Air Museum visitors can inspect another C-3, NC17449, one of a handful of survivors from the 205 built by the Aeronautical Corp of America

Above Dawn and a Lockheed 12, up for sale at '88's Sun 'n Fun. With polished metal skin, executive seating for eight, King radios and modern avionics, this 1936 masterpiece from James Gerschier was a snip at $32,000

Right Many a modest antique and classic sitting quietly on the grass belies the epic flight made to reach Lakeland. Kevin Miles flew this 1941 Culver Cadet to '88's fly-in across the width of the American continent from Grady, Arizona to attend. With a 90 hp Franklin for power this all-wood design by the now legendary Al Mooney, built with the backing of Walter Beech at Wichita in the early 1940s, was one of several aircraft to use the name Cadet, one now coined yet again for Stuart Millar's Piper trainer (developed from the Cherokee) and the latest Robin club trainer

A hybrid Cessna 195 with clipped-wings, tip tanks and modified engine
installation, cowling and VP three-bladed prop—one of the many 'big' Cessnas
to be found with the 433 classics and antiques that registered in 1989

Molt Taylor's futuristic idea for combining the speed and convenience of flying and solving the problem of mobility once you get to your destination airport: the Aerocar 1. His company Aerocar Inc began development work in 1948 and the prototype flew in October 1949, powered by a Lycoming O–290 located in the car 'pod' driving a pusher-prop mounted on the tip of the tail through an extended drive shaft. Several were built in the early 1950s, but series production never materialized. Taylor is a most respected and knowledgeable proponent of homebuilt aircraft, having designed the Coot amphibian, Imp, Mini-Imp and Bullet—all utilizing the same pusher 'methodology' as the Aerocar. Today, a much more sophisticated Aerocar based on the Honda CRX has de-mountable wings and tail and is powered by a 420 hp Allison turbine engine. Despite being well past normal retirement age, Taylor is working hard on plans to market kits of his CRX, which is expected to cruise at 173 mph when airborne

Above Although the GC-1 forerunner of the Globe Swift was designed in 1941 and two pre-production prototypes built, the next prototype didn't fly until January 1945 because the Globe Aircraft Corporation's resources were fully utilized during WW2 building Beech AT-10's and Curtiss C-46s. The prototypes were built of Bakelite-bonded plywood, but more conventional all-metal construction was employed for all subsequent Swifts. *Ol Blue*, one of 1502 Swifts built, has been reworked with a 210 hp engine, tip tanks, a metalized paint job and many other refinements. The Swift has been a popular aircraft with US sport pilots and an increasing number have been similarly customized. Perhaps it was this that inspired Stuart Millar and his Piper company to employ the talents of Roy LoPresti to build and market the Swiftfury, a 200 hp Textron Lycoming IO-360-powered version for the 1990s. When Millar announced at 1988's Sun 'n Fun that he was to put the Piper Cub back into production, rumours were rife about the Swift project, but he wouldn't be drawn on the subject. Sure enough at 1989's Sun 'n Fun the first Swiftfury was displayed and orders flooded in both during and after the show. The Swift is here to stay

Canadian Clipper is far from it: based at Summerland Key, Florida with J L Rogers, is this Grumman G-44 Widgeon. Essentially a scaled down version of the G-21 Goose, Widgeons served as sub-spotters with the US Navy in WW2, designated J4F-1

Showtime

Right 'N34', the FAA's restored DC-3, is a Sun 'n Fun regular, part of a large 'Fed' presence at the show. Originally built in 1945, she served with the US Navy for 18 years in places such as Rome, Paris, Baghdad and Cairo before being assigned to FAA duties in 1963 for flight checking and calibration of navigational aids. In 1985 plans to scrap her were abandoned and she was restored to airworthy condition

Below Piedmont swansong in 1988, when their pristine DC-3 graced the Lakeland turf. It was the fortieth anniversary of Piedmont's first revenue earning flight in February 1948 when a DC-3 flew between Wilmington and Cincinnati—and the end of an era because Piedmont, for so long fiercely independent and partisan, had been taken over by USAir and was soon to lose its unique identity

With a squeak of tyres and a puff of smoke N44V, the beautifully restored DC-3 in Piedmont Airlines livery touches down at 1988's Sun 'n Fun. This particular aircraft never flew with Piedmont, although N44V was the number of the fifth DC-3 the airline acquired in 1948. N44V was bought from Basler Flight Services at Oshkosh to help celebrate the carrier's big 'four-zero' and to perform promotional work at airshows and airports throughout the Piedmont 'patch', frequently being flown by retired Piedmont captain Bill Kyle. However, Piedmont were concerned that folks who weren't familiar with the airline would think that the carrier was still using DC-3s on its scheduled services . . .

Leo Loudenslager might sound a contrived name for someone flying a Laser
200 sponsored by a light beer company. Loudenslager, born in Columbus, Ohio
in 1944, is one of the USA's top aerobatic pilots and was World Aerobatic
Champion in 1980 flying this aircraft in front of the home crowd when that
year's championships were held at Oshkosh. His aircraft is a much modified
Stephens Akro — with a new wing, revised aerofoil, raised turtledecks, faired in
canopy, cleaned up rudder, enlarged tailplane and considerable lightening of the
airframe. After three changes of spinner, five props, three cowlings, two
forward fuselages, three turtledecks, two new wings and two tails before the
final configuration was arrived at. Any resemblance to the original Akro is

Inset, left Montaine Mallet and his wife are 'The French Connection'. The aeronautical connection is their pair of French designed and built Mudry CAP-10 aerobatic monoplanes

Left Settled down in the shade of wings or out in the open but with plenty of barrier cream, the crowd thrills to Montaine Mallet, half of 'The French Connection', as he barrel rolls his CAP-10 with smoke on

Above right Military participation is not huge but is certainly active and varied. In 1989 this Navy Beechcraft T-44A from Corpus Christi, Texas—a military version based on the well known King Air C90 and part of a batch of 61 supplied as advanced multi-engined pilot trainers—added to the colour

Below right When their spraying days are over Piper Pawnee cropdusters still have plenty of life left, be it for glider tugging or pure sport flying. This was one of a pair of brightly coloured Pawnees which flew in on the last day of 1987's Sun 'n Fun

Above From much colder climates in Canada and still wearing its wheel skis, a Polish PZL-104 Wilga provides an unusual sight at 1988's Sun 'n Fun. The 860 examples built since 1962 have been exported to 26 countries

Left This patriotic DHC-3 Otter spends most of its time hauling sky-divers aloft, as many as 15 at a time, before depositing them into Florida skies

Richard VanGrunsven in his latest RV design, the RV-6A, a tri-gear version of
the tail-dragger RV-6. To help pilots find their parking spot again after a flight
from Lakeland, the EAA have thoughtfully provided row numbers at the edge
of the taxyway: homebuilts and classics to the left and 'spams' to the right

Splash-In

Left *Thunder Duck*, a Warner Anderson EA-1 Kingfisher homebuilt amphibian, comes down off the step of the hull and ploughs slowly to its mooring on the shores of Lake Parker, largest of the local lakes from which Lakeland gets its name, to attend the Seaplane Pilots Association Splash-In

Above Each year during the last Friday of Sun 'n Fun week the aquatic visitors to the fly-in make a (sea) bee-line for Lake Parker, about ten miles to the northeast of Lakeland airport on the other side of town. Down on the lake floatplanes, seaplanes and amphibians mingle amongst the reeds, waterfowl and reptiles in an idyllic and refreshing setting after the hurly-burly of Sun 'n Fun. The fly-in has been held every year since 1979

Stepping gingerly ashore from his Lake Buccaneer is one of Florida's best known seaplane characters, Jon Brown. It was his father, Jack Brown, who set up the now internationally known Jack Brown's Seaplane Base at nearby Winterhaven, one of the few commercial schools for training seaplane pilots in the world. Now with a fleet of float-equipped Piper Cubs and Cessna 172s, this Lake Buccaneer and a unique United Consultant's Corp Twin-Bee, Jon carries on the work started by his father. If Jon's lucky he won't get his feet wet!

The Seaplane Pilots Association (SPA) have arrived, the western shore of Lake Parker being the mooring spot for anything up to 40 assorted aircraft from float-equipped ultralights to Grumman twins. At 1987's Splash-In SPA members were jubilant after the announcement of a major judicial decision in their favour—an attempt had been made to prevent seaplanes landing on all but a few inland lakes and waterways in Florida. They won the right to splash down on any lake in the State

Nosing in through the reeds on the shores of Lake Parker, another Republic RC-3 SeaBee joins in the fun at the SPA Splash-In. The basic SeaBee has a pusher 215 hp Franklin 6A8 engine—another visitor to the lake was the TwinBee from Jack Brown's Seaplane Base. Modified by United Consultants Corporation, this SeaBee has two conventional wing-mounted 180 hp Lycomings

Forget the grass, let's get some of that water beneath our feet as a Republic SeaBee starts up ready for the short flight to Lake Parker and some splashing about. Check the gear is down for a land arrival, check its retracted for a water arrival, and if you intend going amphibian after a water landing, check the gear is down and locked before making landfall

125

Above Leaving the lake behind its time to retract those wing-tip floats as Bill Rose heads his Goose back to Lakeland airport. Rose runs a packaging business in Barrington, Illinois but also has a winter base at Marco Island, Florida from where he can keep an eye on his restaurant business

Right Rose's G-21A, N600ZE, s/n B-100, is one of 43 registered in the US in 1988, and was originally built in 1944 as one of the 190 JRF-5's built for the US Navy. The Goose was converted in 1969 by McKinnon Enterprises Inc of Sandy, Oregon with the fitment of advanced wing/flap devices and retractable floats

Downtown—junction of Memorial and Florida, en route to the EAA's next
exciting Sun 'n Fun